Tales from Happyville

Martin Copilah

VANTAGE PRESS
New York

Illustrated by Janet Kucharnik

FIRST EDITION

Published by Vantage Press, Inc.
516 West 34th Street, New York, New York 10001

Manufactured in the United States of America
ISBN: 0-533-10893-4

Library of Congress Catalog Card No.: 93-94971

0 9 8 7 6 5 4 3 2 1

To my daughter, Jehana

To my Teacher
from Jehana .

To Shelly, happy Reading !!!

To [signature] 05/15/'96.

Contents

Introduction

Welcome to Happyville. Please leave your nightmares outside. Here only beautiful thoughts become reality. No one is untrue. People and dragons are themselves, and magic is in abundance. It is a place of fun and excitement where dwarves, and fairies, dragons, and friendly prehistoric beings live in harmony. So read on and find yourself amidst beautiful creatures that do exist . . . if only you would allow them.

Tales from Happyville

1
Eggy and Kangy Invent the "Stomp"

Just before twelve noon, in a land pretty close to far away, lived Eggy the dragon. A pretty cultured dragon, Eggy enjoyed his dish of pebbles and leaves, sometimes varied with leaves and pebbles. Such a diet had little or no disastrous effect on his moods. A gentle and peaceful dragon, he only blew smoke through his nostrils to ward off pesky mosquitoes from denting their proboscises on his scales. Any sensible dragon would avoid harming another creature and Eggy was a sensible dragon.

One day a kangasaurus came to live in Happyville, where Eggy had taken up residence. Kangasauruses are horrid big

KANGY BABY

floppy-eared creatures who delight in stepping on other species' toes. Their diet consists chiefly of stamped marshmallows and sea water, which made Happyville, with its mountains of marshmallows and beautiful beaches, a perfect choice. No two kangasauruses can live in the same place since they would step on each others' toes for centuries until one of their feet became extinct. Thus they have been given credit for a popular dance called the "monster mash."

Trouble was bound to visit at 1:00 P.M., with the kangasaurus setting up cave in Eggy's turf.

> "Sunshine on the pebble
> Sunshine on the trees
> I'm going to eat these, these and 'these?' "

Here Eggy paused, considering a particularly huge pebble with the words "Kangy Baby" carved on it. "What on earth is Kangy Baby? The Graffitti Mavericks should not have done that!"

For those who have never been to

Happyville, Graffitti Mavericks are a group
of dragons and others who ravage the
countryside, writing such things as "Puff
was here," "M.R. has knobby knees,"
"Einstein has fleas," and "Henri dyes his
scales" but never "Kangy Baby."

Eggy sat. He always did when faced
with a problem. These days he found
himself sitting so often that the scales on
his hind quarters shone. He tried not to
think too hard since it made his scales
tingle, but "Kangy Baby" was a tough rock
to place.

"Oh shucks, it's probably not good anyway.
Why should I stay?
I'll go and play."

With that he turned to stomp off and
that's when he discovered the crater.
Falling was one of those hateful things (it
often happened when he forgot to step over
his tail) and falling into a crater was not a
very pleasant experience. He need not have
worried about breaking his tail since he had
a nice warm cushiony sleeping
Kangasaurus to land on.

Kangasauruses, it should be noted, live in a huge hole called a crater, which they dig by jumping up and down with their feet pointed like ballet dancers. They had once migrated to the moon, after a crafty Astrophagus Travel Agency convinced them that the Moon had lots of sea water, as well as cheese-flavoured marshmallows. Having finished all the cheese-flavoured marshmallows and finding no sea water to quench their thirst, they returned, leaving behind huge craters and footprints that would later baffle men. Needless to say, the Astrophagus moved to Mars where he makes a living by selling stamped visas to hitchhikers in space.

"EEEPS! What on Happyville is thisss?" screamed Kangy Baby.

Kangasauruses never expect visitors to drop in. Thus, their one room is built specifically to accommodate one kangasaurus and is quite comfortable unless one has a dragon as big as oneself standing on one. This was Kangy Baby's predicament, one he predicted would end soon.

"Get off my chestsss, you overgrown lizardsss!" he exclaimed. "What are you doing in earth . . . ?"

"You oversized fur coat?" Eggy politely queried.

"Soon as I can get ups, I will step on your toesiesss," Kangy promised. His promise went unheeded by Eggy, who was busy looking for buttons on his new discovery. Needless to say, Eggy had never met a kangasaurus and had only heard stories of them by his grandfather Puff. These he found as hard to believe as the ones about the children of men being nice and friendly.

While looking for buttons with his tail, Eggy encountered some sharp zipper-looking objects that nipped his hitherto unblemished tail.

"Yipes! Yipes! Yipes!
That's not nice."

Eggy belted this out while bolting out. Having reached the top of the crater, Eggy paused, consoling his bruised tail by cooing softly to it. "You poor, poor thing. . . . Soon you'd be healing."

All the while, the troubled Eggy peered into the crater. Did he imagine it? Did it nip him with its zip? Had he spent too much time in the moat? Was there a voice from the overgrown fur coat?

Meanwhile Kangy had gotten very annoyed and was shaking his shaggy fist at Eggy. "You will pay for thisss, you stationary chameleon."

With that thought in mind he decided that he must step on Eggy's toes before he made his one-story crater any bigger (that's because all this time he was jumping up and down with his toes pointed like a ballet dancer). So he jumped out of his crater and landed toe to toe with Eggy.

"Now you will seesss," he cried menacingly, moving away from Eggy. "I'm going to jump up and down your toesss!"

Eggy was not at all pleased with this. Having an overgrown fur coat jump up and down on one's feet did not sound like fun. Anyway it was 1:15 P.M. and time for his afternoon nap, and he was already bored with his new discovery, who had walked so far away that he could no longer see him.

Contrary to popular belief, dragons do not return to their caves after lunch for a siesta. It is too much trouble. They simply fall asleep wherever and whenever they finish lunch. If one walked through Happyville after 1:15 P.M. one could see lots and lots of dragons asleep. Some with their heads in the spring making the water bubble, posterior pointing heavenwards. Others had their heads in the trees, unchewed leaves falling out while others were in midbite, rocks dangling precariously from their mouths (n.b., never disturb a sleeping dragon; it is hazardous to your health and may cause hair loss).

Another thing about dragons, especially young dragons is that they can't stand boredom. Once they are bored they simply fall asleep. Once, a couple of times back, someone suggested they elect a leader of dragons (I think it was Eggy's great-grand-uncle). Anyway, by the time the concept was verbalized, everyone was fast asleep, and since no one seconded the motion it was never passed.

Eggy suffered from both conditions, boredom and after-lunch sleepiness. So by the time Kangy had covered enough distance for his run up to jump on Eggy's toes, Eggy was fast asleep. If a kangasaurus is mad at someone, he goes for miles to take a run-up before jumping on the person's toes. That is how the Astrophagus who tricked them into going to the moon was able to make his getaway (they had gone a couple of miles to take a run-up so he was able to say good-bye to all his relatives, known and unknown, before leaving for Mars).

Kangasauruses have this way of stepping on people's toes—they jump and while in midair they turn their backs on their victims so that they land heels first on their victim's toes.

Kangy knew very little about dragons, and ignorance can be very painful at times. For instance, any old dweller in Happyville knows that stepping on a dragon's toenails is an electrifying experience, even if the dragon has had a manicure recently. Eggy hated manicures. He had decided long ago to let it all hang out (it was an instant trend with the younger ones, although the older and more conservative wagged their tails at it).

Z-Z-Z-Z
BURP

At the precise moment that Kangy landed on Eggy's toes, Eggy burped. When a dragon burps, it is not just hot air. It is usually accompanied by some fire. So Kangy was not only affected by Eggy's electrifying toenails but also by the flames that set his shaggy posterior alight.

"EEEKSSS!!!" Kangy bellowed as he leapt from Eggy's toes. While stomping to cool his feet, he swung his hands vigourously to put out his burning posterior, all the time moving farther and farther away from Eggy. That is when the Brontosaurus B.C., a swinging rock group, noticed him. They had moved to the open air to practice for the night's concert.

"Groovy, Monster, groovy!!"

"Dig those moves. Wild, Monster, really wild!" were the cheers that Kangy got.

"OWWSSS, OWWSSS, OWWSSS!!" Kangy screamed.

Great lyrics, the group thought. So they included them in their new song, which went:

"She loves you
OWWSSS, OWWSSS, OWWSSS,

She loves you
OWWSSS, OWWSSS, OWWSSS,
She loves you
And you know you can't be me!"

This group had had such hits as "Monster Figure," "On the Wings of Dragee," "Where Do Astrophagus Go," "Don't Look Back, There Is a Man on Your Back." That night they also included Kangy's dance, which is what they thought it was, in their concert performance.

So when Eggy attended the concert dressed in his polka dot bow tie and jams, he was much impressed. He had little idea that he and his friend Kangy (they had become distant friends by this time) had invented the dance that the Brontosaurus B.C. had patented as "The Stomp." The dance was quite a hit and quickly spread to other worlds, including Earth where it was later called rock and roll, da butt, and the twist.

Needless to say Kangy avoided stepping on others' feet, especially Eggy's, and Eggy is careful not to fall into Kangy's crater.

2
The Critic

There lived an old woman in Happyville. Of course many old women lived in Happyville; it was indeed a perfect place for old women. It was quiet and peaceful even after Kangy and Eggy invented the Stomp. You see, most of the inhabitants of Happyville lived in soundproof caves and there were no streets to cross, the mode of transport being air . . . dragons and floaters. Brings to mind the time there was a price-slashing war between the dragons and floaters and then Kangy got into business . . . but that's another story. Let's talk about the old woman.

Like all old women, this old woman was special. The typical fairy grandmother type (actually she was an old fairy) who could wish up a batch of cookies before your stomach could grumble twice. Anyway, she had this problem. She called a spade a

spade even if it shovelled out of her path.
She told everybody her opinion about
anything, even if they were not listening.
She told the cats their whiskers were too
long. She told Eggy his scales were on the
wrong way and that when he slept he
looked like an overfed lizard. She told
Kangy that he behaved almost human. She
was a critic.

Now the residents of Happyville are an
easy-going folk who partied to celebrate
success and partied to ward off depression
from failure. Constructive criticism was
welcomed, but nagging was frowned upon
and effectively banned following an incident
involving Worrita, the old woman whom
this story is about.

Our tale begins with Worrita taking a
ride on a floater out to Gooseberry Woods.
She was going to collect berries for the

famous Berry of Berries celebration, which is held in Happyville to celebrate the beginning of the berry season, the end of the berry season, and somewhere in the middle of the berry season.

Floaters, as everybody is aware of in Happyville, know Happyville like the back of their hands. Actually, the back of a floater's hand does look like an aerial view of Happyville. Anyway, Worrita insisted that since she was paying the floater for transport, he should follow her directions. Payment in Happyville consists of hugs and thank you's. A trip from Worrita's cottage to Gooseberry Woods would cost about two hugs and one thank you.

Here is a rundown of Worrita's trip. First she criticized the floater for not bringing a sofa on his back so that she could relax on her flight. When they eventually got to Gooseberry Woods, she chided him for not reminding her to bring a bag for the berries. Somewhere in between she insisted that the floater float under a raincloud that happened to be in the neighbourhood. Floaters, everybody knows, can see through rain clouds, or any cloud for that matter. Since he was following Worrita's directions, she had to see. The result? They got properly well-drenched, and the floater got slippery. Worrita slid off and had to flutter her wings as quickly as possible to get back on.

They also ended up somewhere in Applesauce Creek because Worrita thought she saw berries growing there. It was such a sticky predicament, and after quite a

delay, the floater took her to Gooseberry
Woods where she quickly gathered berries
in her apron. By the time they got back, the
Berry of Berries celebration was already in
progress. To make up for the trouble she
had caused, Worrita paid the floater
double—two thank yous and four hugs.

Worrita hurriedly made her famous
gooseberry pies, which everybody looked
forward to having at every Berry of Berries
celebration. But, alas, they were not as
good as before. Worrita, in her haste, had
left out her secret magic spell, which made
them crumbly and soft. Instead, they were
almost as hard as Eggy's toenails. Everyone
went home disappointed and with a serious
jaw pain, even Bronty, who at one time had

eaten Kangy's steel trap door, mistaking it for a shellfish.

An urgent meeting was held the next day by the town's wisemen, who reluctantly gave up their tic-tac-toe tournament scheduled for that same day. A resolution was passed. It read:

> Nobody under any circumstances is permitted to criticize somebody's performance of something which they themselves could not do as well or better.

The interesting thing was that no one had any grounds for criticism. Criticism was then replaced by a pat on the back in Happyville.

Bonk

3
Look Out, Rocksters!

It was way past June in Happyville and all was quiet around Ignore, the village storyteller. Today Ignore was enticing his audience with a tale of fairylike creatures (they looked more like rocks to me) who were called the Rocksters. These creatures had accidentally floated into Happyville many moons past and had made it their home. This was a fact that they and most other Happyville citizens knew little or nothing about. However, if it was mentioned, they were bound to say, "Oh, I remember."

"I was wandering on my way to Happyville," Ignore droned on. The road to Happyville is a straight one. Ignore, on the other hand, wanders wherever he goes. If you ever see a short, old, stumpy dwarf, with beard sweeping the road, walking in a zig-zag fashion, that would be Ignore. You

25

had better lock up all your chocolate chip cookies and prepare yourself for an unbelievable story, like the one he was just telling.

"I was wandering up the road when I noticed two huge black balls following me, but they were having difficulty keeping up since every now and then they bumped into trees I was carefully avoiding."

Here he paused to let the suspense sink in. "I have seen many strange things in my time but never huge black balls floating in my wake. Indeed, once I saw a brown furry ball snoring in its sleep and muttering, 'When I get my feet on that Eggy . . .' Anyway, enough of that. Eventually, they caught up with me. I paused in midstride, wondering whether I should continue the way my nose was pointed or double back and surprise them. I kept my eyes glued in front not daring to look back, since my nose would then be pointed in the opposite direction."

Here Ignore paused rather long, waiting to see how much his audience was interested in his story. Generally an entire story could cost up to twelve chocolate chip cookies. Of course his audience was interested so they all chipped in and he got eleven cookies. Contented, he continued. "I held my walking stick firmly in my hand." (I guess if he did not, it would probably have walked away. Once he was telling a particularly boring story. It was about a man who changed his entire personality when he took off his glasses. His walking stick got up and took a couple of steps away and he had to walk as fast as his little legs could carry him to retrieve it.)

"*Oh*, I thought, *so they think they've caught up with me. Well, I'll take off so fast it will make them dizzy.* As I was poised to do just that, a kind voice boomed out, 'Howdy-doo, Dwarfy?' *Well*, I thought, *anyone who knows the family must be a friend.* So without turning around and

while taking a few unhurried steps, I said,
'I'm fine, thank you. And you?'

" 'Just hanging around,' was the reply.
'We are visiting our cousins in Happyville
and since you are a Happyvillian, we were
following you.' "

"Cousins in Happyville! Are they here
still?" Eggy screamed.

"What on Earth is thisss you sayss?"
Kangy nervously queried.

Ignore never liked being disturbed or
sidetracked when he was telling a story,
and he never is. Once he was telling a story
of some Kangasaurus's flight to the moon to
some well-fed dragons in the barn. Needless
to say, one burped and the house went up in
flames. While the villagers threw buckets of
water to put out the flames, he finished the
story, walking out all covered in soot, half
his beard burnt, muttering, ". . . so the
Astrophagus moved to the moon where he
makes his life selling . . ." He then
demanded his cookies and was paid. He is
such a dedicated storyteller.

So he continued as though Eggy and
Kangy had never spoken. "Of course, I

knew nothing of their cousins in Happyville
but not wanting to be considered a dunce, I
pretended that the idea was not new to me
and we proceeded along our merry way. For
want of something to say [which is rather
strange since Ignore always has something
to say] I introduced myself, bowing politely
and modestly informing them that I,
Ignore, am the greatest storyteller in the
universe. They should have heard of me
from their cousins in Happyville, but they
pretended not to remember. One was called
Igneous the first and the other Rocky the
twenty-fifth. Igneous was the older of the
two and thus more composed."

With that Ignore promptly began to eat
his chocolate chip cookies, which signalled
that the story was over. There were many
cries of dismay, many "ooohss" and "umpss"
as distressed citizens asked for a refund.
Eggy and Kangy were particularly
displeased with this story. It was too short,
too unbelievable, and to top it all off,
neither had ever encountered a rockster in
their years in Happyville. This is not hard
to understand, as rocksters never make

friends unless absolutely necessary. Of course, they had been lost and had to accompany Ignore for their own reasons.

Ignore refused to refund the chocolate chip cookies since he reasoned that they could not refund his story. Clearly upset, Eggy decided to fly and shake the cobwebs from his wings. Kangy decided to join him. Of course, kangasauruses do not have wings like dragons. They do not have wings at all. So how did Kangy keep up with Eggy? Well, kangasauruses can jump so high and for so long that it can sometimes be mistaken for flying.

Eggy decided to fly to the island of Bettyberg, where his aunt Bettyberg was the sole inhabitant. She was an old recluse with little time for anyone except her favorite nephew Eggy. Ever since he had almost wrecked her cave upon testing her chilli rocks, which inspired him to jump around singing "Hot Rocks" (a song by Brontosaurus B.C.), she had taken to calling him pet names like clumsy oaf and a bag of scales. It conveyed a lot of emotion.

It was only in midair that Kangy

realized where Eggy was headed. By then it was too late and there was nothing he could do. The island of Bettyberg is some distance off the coast of Happyville, which was a little too far for Kangy to jump. He would have to make a stop somewhere before Bettyville, and that meant the ocean.

Panic overtook Kangy, especially since he was slowing down and the ocean looked cold and promising. It did not make any sense yelling to Eggy since he was so far away and dragons make quite a lot of noise while in flight.

"I hopess I don't landsss on those rockss! I'll keep my toess crossess!" But as Kangy fell lower and lower, he became hopelessly certain that he would land on those rocks. The rocks loomed closer and closer and even though he balled himself the rocks kept coming at him.

Waits a minutess, he thought, *I'm not justs falling towards them, they are risings towards me!! ROCKSTERS!!* The thought struck terror into his heart, and he crossed his toes even tighter.

SPLASH
SPLISH
SPLOOSH

"What's up?" queried Igneous the first on catching up with (or was it down?) with Kangy.

"I'm going downss. That's what's upss!!" screamed Kangy.

While Igneous pondered this understatement, Kangy fell closer and closer to the ocean, followed by four identified flying objects. Igneous the first, Rocky the twenty-fifth, and their two cousins from Happyville, Metamorphic Three and Pebbles Two all followed Kangy. These four are not always identified. Indeed, once while visiting California (they had gone to pick up a sun tan) they were referred to as UFOs (unidentified floating objects) by the people there. Needless to say that it was Pebbles Two with her saucerlike shape that gave rise to the rumours about the flying saucers.

In Happyville, flying saucers even pots and pans are a regular thing. I too have had close encounters with them while visiting my married friend there, but that is another story.

Kangy hit the ocean with a big splash, although he was certain that the ocean had

Z-Z-Z
Z-Z-Z-Z

hit him. The Rocksters were all soaked with water, something that they loved. Indeed, they often splashed into the ocean as Kangy had just done. *He must be a fun guy,* they all thought. So they decided to join in. Kangy was just catching his breath from his encounter with the ocean when he heard a deafening "Kabong!" as the Rocksters dove into the ocean simultaneously.

With great haste Kangy swam for the island of Bettyberg, followed by the Kabonging of the Rocksters who accompanied him. Eggy was surprised to see his friend show up dripping wet at his aunt's place, looking terrified and telling an even more terrifying story. Eggy found it all very hard to believe. By the time Kangy had six cups of hot chocolate fudge, they were both sleepy. So they spent the night resting in Aunt Bettyberg's cave, remembering how they had met and promising each other to be friends even if the concrete and the rocks beneath their feet began to chase them.